THE REDEMPTION MOVEMENT

THE REDEMPTION MOVEMENT

Deliverance for Black America

Wade L Jackson

ISBN-13: 9780996479202
ISBN-10: 0996479201

This book is dedicated to all the parents who, regardless of personal circumstances, will raise their children to be the best that they can be and will ensure that their children begin adulthood fully or near fully prepared and with little to no negatives or bad habits.

Contents

1

Introduction

We as black people have a tremendous opportunity before us at this point in time. We can do something great for ourselves. We can solve or eliminate most of the larger problems facing black Americans as a societal group. It does not require governmental or political action or demonstrations. It does not require fund-raising or contributions from businesses, other organizations, or individuals. It is 100 percent self-determined and not subject to the whims, ideas, or approval of any outside group or individual.

I know that making such a bold statement would prompt most people to ask, "Now, who are you to make such statement?" I am not a familiar writer, a celebrity, or a noted civil rights person. I am not looking to make money or achieve fame. (In fact, I fully expect this project to cost me money.) This is not about me. It's all about "we, the black people."

Here is a brief summary of who I am just so you'll know a few things about me. However, your attention and emphasis must remain on the ideas and proposals presented herein, not on me.

I have always been attentive to the lives of African Americans. Growing up in Aiken County, South Carolina, in the 1940s, 1950s, and early 1960s', white/black issues were inescapable. I attended a one-room, one-teacher, first-to-third-grade grammar school that had no electricity and one wood-burning heater. Later, I had to walk over two miles each way to attend elementary school—rain or shine, hot or cold. On the way to and from school, we were passed by white children on school buses. Our school-books were mostly ones that had been used by white children.

In 1953 my family moved, and I began attending Jefferson Elementary School. It was a newer, recently built brick school with many modern facilities and equipment. We also had school buses. This was a much better learning situation. In 1956 a high school, Jefferson High School, was added on to this school. The new and improved schools were primarily the response of the South Carolina Board of Education to avoid integration brought on by the *Brown v. Board of Education* case and previous legal actions by Thurgood Marshall and other NAACP attorneys. Although the schools were still segregated, we were in much better learning conditions, with good teachers who took personal interests in the students.

There were many exciting (and scary) things happening in the mid-1950s and early 1960s. In May 1954 the Supreme Court issued the decision in the *Brown v. Board of Education* case that struck down the 1896 *Plessy v. Ferguson* decision that had legalized separate-but-equal segregation. In late 1955 Rosa Parks refusing to give up her seat in the black section of the bus to a white man led to the subsequent Montgomery, Alabama, bus boycott. In 1956 Martin Luther King Jr. emerged during the Montgomery bus boycott and became a very powerful and commanding national leader for blacks. In early 1960 North Carolina A&T students began sit-ins at white-only lunch counters in Greensboro, North Carolina. Related, black music was inspirational and wonderful. We had become very hopeful for the future. It was a wonderful and exciting time to be young and black.

From the fall of 1961 to the spring of 1965, I attended college at Tuskegee University in Tuskegee, Alabama. It was a blessed experience. What a wonderful way to transition from a teenage high school graduate to an adult out on my own. The educational, cultural, and social growth in college was very good. At that same time, The Civil Rights Movement moved into high gear. Some of the highlights were the August 1963 march on Washington, DC, and the Martin Luther King Jr. "I Have a Dream" speech; the 1964 Civil Rights Act signed into law in July 1964; and the

Voting Rights Act signed into law in August 1965. I continued to follow the movement after college.

I graduated in May 1965 with a bachelor of science (BS) in mechanical engineering and began my working career in the space industry in June 1965. I noticed one key thing right away. Supervisors and coworkers would tell me what to do, usually from a distance and with little to no explanation, while they would sit with and show new whites hires what to do and spend a lot of time with them to make sure they understood and did things correctly. I recognized early on that this would not work out well for me. Although it made them uncomfortable, I would insist that they show me also. Fortunately, I was usually faster and better at understanding and doing things, thus making it easier for them to help me. I continued to work and study, becoming a registered professional engineer in February 1971 and receiving a master of business administration (MBA) in June 1971.

As my career continued, I became primarily a design engineer. Quite often I was assigned the more difficult problems that others were unable to solve. Not only would I identify the root-cause problems, I would design, demonstrate, and implement the solutions in a timely and cost-effective manner. The problem solving somehow came easily to me, and I enjoyed it as well. I consider it a blessing from God.

I must point out here that problem solving is not a matter of genius, although this could help. It is more about being open-minded, observant, insightful, objective, disciplined, determined, and visionary. And yes, simple is usually better.

The problems of blacks in America today are the most interesting, most challenging, most important, and potentially the most rewarding that I have ever considered. In the mid- to late-1970s, as The Civil Rights Movement had ended and the Black Power era was nearing its end, I thought that we should have started another new movement—something more self-determined. But as I look back, I see that we needed the time to just engage in the normal American system. Most blacks were very hopeful for their futures within the normal system at that time. However, over time we realized that the system was not working well for most blacks. This new movement that I'm proposing is self-determined and perfectly timed. I truly believe that together we can solve all the problems in a very efficient, effective, and timely manner and also enjoy the journey and the rewards.

In the interests of full disclosure, I must say that I am completely independent. I do not represent any company, organization, ideology, or individual. I am, however, a Baptist Christian, a member of Old Macedonia Baptist Church in North Augusta, South Carolina, and a progressive Democrat. But I've addressed the problems from the best objective and most effective solution approach.

ABOUT THIS BOOK

This book has two main purposes. The first is to present and analyze a potentially powerful national movement that will solve our major problems. The second is to impress that, regardless of how good the idea may be, the most important thing is to actually implement it.

Chapter 2 is about the present and future of black America. Many people are impressed with statistics, which are actually about the past. But our work should be about the future and what we can and should become.

Chapter 3 is a review of our history. This is something that we can be very proud of—yes, proud—and also use as motivation for the future. James Weldon Johnson's poem and song, "Lift Every Voice and Sing," is very touching, especially the lines, "We have come over a way that with tears has been watered. / We have come, treading our path through the blood of the slaughtered." This is so true.

Chapter 4 is about what adults should do to become the best people they can be and what children should do to prepare for adult life to become the best they can be.

Chapter 5 lays out how to become the best people we can be. This is where the need for a movement is discussed.

Chapter 6 is about the essential things of the movement and how to get the movement started successfully.

2

The Present and Future
of Black America

When we think of the present state of black America, it is difficult to say what exactly it is. It can be a reflection of current events, current opinions, and current statistics. Statistics (demographics) that are measured and, hopefully, scientifically determined are more generally accepted as the answer. The US Census Bureau, US Centers for Disease Control, and US Bureau of Labor Statistics are great and reliable sources of statistics. Income, employment, education, wealth, households, health, population, crime, and poverty are the more indicative statistics.

Understanding and interrupting statistics can be quite daunting, especially when placed in context. In summary, however, blacks are lagging badly in median income, employment, educational attainment, household wealth, and home ownership. We have the highest rate of crime and poverty. (For those interested in the details and numbers for these statistics, I refer you to the websites of blackdemographics.com and the three above US bureaus.) In context, it can be unfair to compare black statistics to white statistics in many areas. Blacks were not on anything like a level playing field until the mid-1970s. Whites have been playing on a level playing field for centuries. So here we are, competing or comparing our statistics with those of people who have had all the advantages forever. Add racial prejudice and discrimination into the mix, and it shows that we're up against a stacked deck and an uphill climb in this comparison.

But comparison should not be our measurement at this point in history. Progress over the last forty years or so since the mid-1970s is our measurement. We have made great progress in education, income, music, sports, and entertainment, but we have regressed very badly in health and family households. Over 50 percent of black adults, both male and female, are quite a bit overweight, and many are obese, with all the side effects: diabetes, heart attacks, strokes, and the need for knee and hip replacements. About 25 percent of black family households with school-age children are headed by single females. This causes child poverty, child discipline problems, low self-esteem, very low household wealth with very little chance of home ownership, and many other related problems.

But we are not our statistics. They are a measure of the past. Our yesterday must not become our tomorrow also. We can create our own desirable future for all blacks, not just the lucky few. How about this future?

1. People of good character and high morals, with good spiritual and religious values
2. People in excellent health. People who eat nutritious and properly prepared food, get regular medical and dental checkups, exercise, and maintain good health
3. People who are good spouses, parents, family members, friends, coworkers, neighbors, and citizens
4. People who are all high school graduates, many with college or professional degrees or vocational certificates
5. People employed in good and well-paying jobs with good future opportunities. Many are self-employed professionals and business owners
6. People with a very high percentage of married-couple family households. Almost all families with children are two-parent households

Does this sound too good or too idealistic to become true? Not really. We all can become just this. With slight but consistent changes in our path, we *will* become this change. Not just the lucky few but all blacks. Yes, *all*! Then we can say:

WE ARE REDEEMED. WE ARE DELIVERED.

More details on how we can become these new people are given in chapters 4, 5, and 6. But next, let's look at our black history.

3

The Path of Our Past

In this chapter we review the times and some of the events that brought us to this point in our history. Our history is rich, beautiful, and captivating, and we should all be proud and study it more. It is not the intent here to present a complete black history and analysis. Also, this is not intended to be a scholarly presentation with citations and footnotes. Some of the books and sources that give good basic historical facts, knowledge, and motivation are listed in the bibliography. Our aim here is to present an easily readable surface view that will be useful to most of the readers of this book. The focus is also on the people as a whole and not so much on individuals.

AFRICA

Although most of us are many generations American born and raised, we are African American for good reason. Many of our souls, rhythms, feelings, instincts, and many other "who we are" characteristics were shaped and determined by many generations of African people. Therefore, the history of Africa is *our* history to some degree. We should be very proud of this. (I must note that as Americans we have many other influences also.)

Africa is the second-largest continent in the world. It is larger than the North American (which contains the United States), South American, or European continents. Currently, in 2013, there are more than fifty countries and over one billion people living in Africa. The continent is rich in oil, gold, diamonds, other minerals, and many other natural resources.

Growing up earlier in the United States, it was very difficult, or more likely impossible, to obtain any accurate knowledge of African history in elementary and secondary schools or in general society. This happened for two reasons: US history is mostly Eurocentric, and the presence and later legacy of slavery and racial discrimination created a need to deny the truth and present untruths about Africa. African history is readily available today.

AFRICAN SLAVE TRADE

Slavery existed in many countries and kingdoms from the beginning of recorded history. Egypt, Greece, Rome, and Israel are some of those countries, just to name a few. African slavery existed among African countries, including Arab countries, especially as the result of war captives. African transatlantic slavery, however, was the longest lasting, most disruptive, most devastating human cruelty in history.

Portugal was the first European country to participate in the African slave trade, beginning in 1444. This was followed by many other European countries, including England in 1562. This trade would continue until the 1870s. During this period it is estimated that more than eight million African slaves were brought to North and South America (including the Caribbean). Additionally, millions of captives died on slave ships, and many thousands more were killed during capture. We refer to this entire system as the murder, kidnapping, forced transporting, human trafficking, and enslavement of African people.

BROAD CHRONOLOGICAL HISTORY OF AFRICAN AMERICANS IN THE BRITISH COLONIES AND SUBSEQUENT UNITED STATES

The history of slavery and Jim Crow segregation in America is shameful and embarrassing, especially to most whites. Most American history writers have all but ignored it. Others try to put a positive spin on it and never, or very briefly, mention the horrors. Still others emphasize the achievements of the few successful blacks and try to pass this off as black history.

Let me be clear. Black history is the history of black people as a whole, not of a few black people (out of millions) who did or are doing well. Unless the black man's or woman's history is so bound up with the history of black people (such as Martin Luther King Jr.), it is just the history of that black person. While we are proud of the accomplishments of any and all blacks, especially when considering the obstacles against them, it is the black *people's* history that is important.

Many blacks, while reading black history, have feelings of anger, shame, inferiority, frustration, uneasiness, revengefulness, being trapped, and other feelings that create a taxing or anxious state of mind to avoid, get away from, or at least minimize exposure to their own history. While this is understandable, it is necessary to fight through the initial bad feelings. Our history is what it is, and it will not change. We must grow to love and appreciate the study and knowledge of our history. Let's make every month Black History Month, not just February.

Starting with the first Africans in the English North American settlement, general historical facts and events in African American history are chronologically summarized by significant time periods. (Note that slavery in the French territory of Louisiana and the Spanish territory of Florida, before they were included in the United States, is also part of our history.) A few of the more significant historical facts or events are given for each time period. Little is written about the history of individuals and various sectors, such as music or sports. Also, free Africans in America during the time of slavery, although important, are not stressed. This section is only intended to give you good overall knowledge and a feel of how we the people arrived at where we are today. If you are very familiar with African American history, you can skim to the ending summary. Otherwise, reading the entire history presented here will give you good basic knowledge.

1619 TO 1774: SLAVERY IN THE BRITISH COLONIES

In August 1619 twenty African slaves, shipped in from South America, were purchased in the English colony of Jamestown, Virginia. The English used the indentured service system, a contract-for-labor system that required the servant to work for several years, usually eight or more, to repay the money advanced by the contractor. At the end of the contract, the servant was freed and given land and some money to transition to independence. The early African slaves entered this indentured service system, and some were able to gain their freedom.

As the English colonies and settlements increased, more Africans were brought into the colonies. Initially, the African and English indentured servants worked side by side, and there was cooperation and socializing between them. The ruling class saw this cooperation and socializing as a threat, and they created rules and laws to stop it.

The need for laborers increased greatly, and the colonists began to make rules and laws to ensure a supply. First, the years that Africans had to serve before attaining freedom were increased, and the conditions for their freedom became more difficult in all the colonies. In 1641 the Massachusetts Colony passed the first law recognizing the condition of slavery. In 1662 the Virginia Colony passed slave-code laws. Many different colonies passed various laws to regulate slavery. By the 1750s the slave laws were in place in all the colonies, and slavery was fully established. They defined a slave as African; as property, not a person; and as a slave for life. A child of a slave mother was also a slave, and a slave had virtually no rights, including the right to learn to read and write.

Some African indentured servants and slaves managed to become free in the colonies. At the start of the American Revolutionary War in 1776, it is estimated that there were about half a million Africans in the colonies. It is estimated that 4 to 5 percent were free, or approximately twenty-three thousand. The free Africans lived in both Northern and Southern colonies.

1775 TO 1789: REVOLUTIONARY WAR AND US CONSTITUTION

By 1770 there was great tension between the colonies and the British Empire. The colonies wanted to become an independent country, and the British were not willing to allow this. This led to the American Revolutionary

War, which began in 1775. African Americans believed the war was an opportunity to earn their freedom by fighting in the war.

Initially, the American Continental army did not want African Americans in their army—free or slave. But the British began offering freedom to slaves who would join their side and fight or serve during the war. As many African American slaves joined the British, the Continental army was forced to change its position and allow African Americans to serve as well. An unknown number of slaves were freed by the British and the new United States, though the number is believed to be very small. Many more slaves used the war to escape to freedom. The war ended in November 1782 when the British surrendered. The war formally ended with the signing of the Treaty of Paris in September 1783.

The new United States declared freedom on July 4, 1776 (Independence Day), with the Declaration of Independence. The first draft of the declaration contained a clause about the horrors of slavery that could have resulted in the abolition of slavery. However, the Southern-state representatives objected, and the clause was omitted from the final declaration. Thus, slavery was not mentioned in the declaration.

In 1787 Congress issued the US Constitution. In the debates during the creation of the Constitution, the question of slavery was one of the hottest issues. The final Constitution, without using the words *slave* or *slavery*, referred to slavery in three places. Article 1, section 2 implies that a slave ("all other persons") shall count as three-fifths of a person for the purpose of determining representatives and taxes. Article 1, section 9 states that the migration or importation and use of slaves ("such persons that any states now existing…think is proper to admit") shall not be prohibited by Congress prior to 1808. Article 4, section 2 states that no slave ("person held to service or labor") shall become free by moving from his slavery-allowed state to a free state. The Constitution was ratified by all thirteen states in 1789.

The American Revolutionary War, Declaration of Independence, and Constitution were very important and beneficial to white Americans, free and indentured. At the time they were of little value and use to African Americans.

1790 TO 1830: SLAVERY EXPANDS IN THE UNITED STATES

The first census taken by the United States was in 1790. There were about 698,000 African American slaves in the country. By 1830 the African American slave population had increased to about two million. Two things happened that were key in this increase: Eli Whitney invented the cotton gin in 1793, and the United States made the Louisiana Purchase in 1803. The cotton gin eliminated all the tedious hand labor required to separate the cotton seeds from the fiber. The Louisiana Purchase doubled the size of the United States at that time. It provided new, southern, fertile land for the growth of cotton and sugar cane. It also influenced the clearing of new lands for cotton in what later became the states of Alabama and Mississippi. Cotton became the largest, most important, and most profitable crop in the United States. As more cotton was planted, more slaves were required. Breeding of slaves was the most economical and popular way used for the slave increase.

In 1808 the United States ended slave importation as was provided for in the Constitution in 1787. Although this theoretically ended slave importation, slave importation actually continued long after this so-called end. During and shortly after the Revolutionary War, most northern states passed laws ending or phasing out slavery. Actually, most of the northern slaves were sold or moved to slaveholding states. Very few slaves were actually freed.

Slaveholders always lived in fear of a slave uprising or revolt. From the beginning there were revolts, escapes, and suicides by slaves. Slaves also burned down homes and poisoned slaveholders. The Second Amendment to the Constitution was about state militias' arms to deal with slave uprisings. In 1791 a slave revolt began in the French Colony of St. Dominguez (now Haiti). This rebellion would ultimately result in a war between the French and the colony and would end in 1804 with the independence of the colony. From the beginning and throughout this conflict, it caused much anxiety and fear among US slaveholders that a similar revolt could or would start in America. Many states enacted unusual laws and actions to address these fears. Two large-scale plots were uncovered that added to this fear: the 1800 Gabriel Prosser plot in Richmond, Virginia, and the Denmark Vesey plot in Charleston, South Carolina.

1830 TO 1860: ABOLITION ERA

This period is referred to as the "abolition era" because the voices and energy for the abolishment of slavery were louder and stronger than ever. There had always been calls for ending slavery, including from the very beginning by the Quakers. But the new voices were louder and more determined than ever before.

There were many great and powerful abolitionists in the 1830s, both black and white. William Lloyd Garrison, Charles Sumner, Reverend Theodore Parker, and Elijah Lovejoy are the more well-known white abolitionists. Frederick Douglass, William Wells Brown, Robert Purvis, Frances Ellen Watkins, Sojourner Truth, and Sarah Parker Remond are the more well-known black abolitionists. These abolitionists held meetings, gave lectures, published pamphlets, and wrote books attacking the institutions of slavery. Frederick Douglass became the most powerful voice for the abolition of slavery.

In the 1820s David Walker, a free northern black, was an activist in the abolition movement. During his lectures and public statements, he called for more militant action and revolts against slavery. In 1829 he published *Walker's Appeal in Four Articles*. It is a scholarly book with some impressive and difficult-to-dispute arguments. Some of the points Walker made in the book were: early Africa and African people laid the foundation for European learning; blacks should be willing to die fighting rather than living as slaves; the white superiority and black inferiority arguments made by Thomas Jefferson and other whites are untrue; how can Americans consider themselves Christians and treat slaves so inhumanely; the Declaration of Independence and Americans' cry for freedom are mockeries; and no black man should leave America for colonization in Africa because we have built this country with our blood and tears. Walker's book enraged and frightened the southern states. It was banned in the South, where it became a crime to own or distribute it.

In August 1831, in the state of Virginia, Nat Turner led the largest slave revolt ever in the United States. They killed sixty-one whites prior to being attacked and scattered by the town militia. Turner was able to escape and avoid capture for many weeks before being captured and hanged. This revolt created widespread panic and various reactions throughout the United States. Many innocent slaves were killed as an act of revenge. States, cities, and towns enacted stricter laws to prevent what many thought was just the beginning of a general slave uprising.

In September 1850 Congress passed the Fugitive Slave Act. This new act required federal officers to arrest any fugitive slave. It required states to turn over anyone accused of being a runaway slave on the mere presentation of an affidavit by the claimant. Accused slaves were not allowed a jury trial, nor were they allowed to testify in their own defense. It was made a crime to give food to or assist a runaway slave in any way. This new law was very unpopular with abolitionists, and many sought to disobey and nullify it. This law also created the consequence of many free blacks being "kidnapped" and sold into slavery. The writing of abolitionist Harriet Beecher Stowe was in opposition to this new law. In 1852 her book, *Uncle Tom's Cabin*, was published and became an instant success. It was the first book written by a white person about the evils of slavery. It created much national and international support for the abolition movement.

In 1857 the Supreme Court issued a decision in the *Dred Scott* case. Dred Scott was a slave who sued for his freedom on the grounds that he had lived in free states for several years. The Supreme Court voted seven to two to deny Scott freedom. The most disturbing thing about the decision may have been the written opinion of Chief Justice Roger B. Taney, a slave owner. He stated that because Scott was black, he was not a citizen of the United States and therefore had no right to sue. He went on further to say that the US Constitution had excluded blacks; they are an inferior race; no blacks could ever become citizens; and blacks had no rights that the white man was required to respect. He also added that the US Congress had no right to limit slavery in any state or territory. His writing upset all abolitionists and all people against the expansion of slavery.

In October 1859 John Brown, a white abolitionist, led a team of whites and blacks in an attack on the US arsenal at Harpers Ferry, Virginia (now West Virginia). His plan was to obtain guns and ammunition, use them to arm slaves, and free other slaves in the area. The state militia and federal troops attacked Brown's group and killed or captured the raiders. Brown was captured and was later hanged. The raid set off new fears among slaveholders because of its interracial nature. John Brown became a folk hero among African Americans.

Slavery was the key issue in the presidential election of 1860. There were four candidates in the race. Illinois Senator Stephen A. Douglas represented the Democratic Party. Vice President John C. Breckinridge of Kentucky was the nominee for the Southern Democratic Party. John Bell of Tennessee was the Union Party nominee. Abraham Lincoln of Illinois was chosen by the Republican Party. Lincoln was well known for wanting to limit the expansion of slavery, and most Southerners considered him an abolitionist. The remaining candidates were compromisers on slavery and its expansion into new territories. Lincoln won the presidency by winning the free states.

The Southern states were convinced that Lincoln and the Republican Party would move to eliminate slavery. In December 1860 South Carolina became the first state to secede from the United States. Six additional Southern states (Alabama, Mississippi, Florida, Georgia, Louisiana, and Texas) also seceded by February 1861. All of these states seceded before the inauguration of Lincoln in March 1861.

1861 TO 1865: CIVIL WAR AND THE ELIMINATION OF SLAVERY

When Lincoln was inaugurated on March 4, 1861, seven Southern slaveholding states had seceded from the Union and established the Confederate States of America as an independent country. The most urgent problem facing Lincoln was how the United States was going to deal with this secession. All along, Lincoln had maintained that he did not want to eliminate slavery in the states where it was already legal. He only wanted to prevent it from spreading to new states and territories. He also wanted to keep the entire Union together.

On April 12, 1861, Confederate soldiers attacked Fort Sumter near Charleston, South Carolina, forcing the federal forces to surrender. This action ultimately resulted in the start of the American Civil War. The Southern slaveholding states of Arkansas, Tennessee, North Carolina, and Virginia seceded and joined the Confederates. The slaveholding states Delaware, Maryland, Kentucky, and Missouri remained loyal to the Union.

From the beginning of the Civil War, African Americans offered to volunteer for service in the Union army but were refused. Also, northern abolitionists exerted pressure on Lincoln from the beginning to free the slaves, but he refused. Lincoln seemed more interested in pleasing the four slaveholding states that remained loyal to the Union. In April 1862 Congress freed approximately three thousand slaves in the District of Columbia by paying the slaveholders about $300 per slave. Lincoln would later make a similar offer to slaveholders in the four slaveholding states in the Union to free their slaves. As the call for complete emancipation of slaves continued, Lincoln reluctantly heeded this call, and in September 1862 he announced that on January 1, 1863, he would issue a proclamation freeing all slaves in the Confederate states. This proclamation would not apply to slaves in states loyal to the Union. On January 1, 1863, this proclamation was issued. This was a very important step in the elimination of slavery.

As the war progressed, blacks began to serve in the Union army and navy in isolated and special situations. As the Union army absorbed heavy losses and fewer whites volunteered for service, Congress approved the recruitment of blacks into the Union army in July 1862. Despite some initial doubt, black soldiers performed a very distinctive service in the war. About two hundred thousand blacks served in the Union army during the war.

On April 9, 1865, the Confederate army surrendered, ending the war. Over six hundred thousand service people were killed during the four-year war. The North lost approximately 350,000 people, 37,000 of whom were black. The South lost approximately 250,000 people. On April 14, 1865, Abraham Lincoln was assassinated.

In January 1865 Congress passed the Thirteenth Amendment to the US Constitution, abolishing all slavery in the United States. On December 6, 1865, the amendment was ratified and officially ended all slavery and indentured service in the United States.

1865 TO 1877: RECONSTRUCTION ERA

The Reconstruction refers to the reintroduction back into the United States of the eleven slaveholding states that fought and lost the American Civil War. There were many economic, political, and social problems to solve. The economy and infrastructure of the South were near complete destruction. There were four million newly freed slaves who were without food, housing, clothing, money, education, or occupation. Many had no family or did not know where family members were. The attitudes and political states of mind of the eleven states were very challenging.

Reconstruction actually started in 1863. When the Union captured a state, Lincoln appointed a military officer to act as governor, and many of the Reconstruction-type problems were being addressed prior to the end of the war. In March 1865 the Freed Bureau was set up by the federal government to provide newly freed slaves with food, clothes, medical attention, housing, education, assistance with obtaining work, and other items of need. Perhaps the greatest work and legacy of the bureau was the establishment of institutions of higher learning for African Americans, some of which still exist today, such as Howard and Fisk Universities.

After the assassination of Abraham Lincoln, Vice President Andrew Johnson became president. Johnson was a son of the South and was sympathetic to Southern policies. Johnson began a quick presidential-only (without Congress) Reconstruction. He pardoned top Confederate officers and returned land captured during the war to the former owners. He negated General Sherman's agreement to give forty acres and a mule to some former slaves living in the low country of South Carolina, Georgia, and Florida. Johnson urged the former Confederate states to elect new governments.

In 1865 and 1866, most Southern former slaveholding states passed what became known as the "Black Codes." The purpose of these laws was to ensure that the South continued to have low-cost labor and to limit the rights and movements of freed blacks. Most Northerners saw the laws as being very similar to the previous slave code laws and would have the effect of essentially returning blacks to slavery. In early 1867 Congress took control of the Reconstruction. They placed the Southern states under military rule and stopped the enforcement of Black Code laws.

After the American Civil War ended, violence against African Americans increased dramatically, especially after blacks began to vote and get elected to political offices. In December 1865 the Ku Klux Klan was formed, and this organization began to assault and kill blacks, who had no protection from local and state police. The Klan grew more powerful and committed so much terror upon blacks that in 1870 Congress passed the Force Acts, making it a federal crime to commit such acts upon any citizen of the United States. The laws were used to arrest and prosecute Klan members for terrorist acts against blacks. Other smaller and local white-terrorist groups were also formed—which included the police in many cases—to use violence and intimidation to keep blacks from voting, holding office, and in general exercising their civil rights. In 1866 Congress passed the Fourteenth Amendment to the Constitution, giving all US citizens equal protection under the law. In 1869 Congress passed the Fifteenth Amendment to the Constitution, giving all US male adult citizens the right to vote. Even with these laws in place, violence continued against blacks during the Reconstruction.

During the US presidential election of 1876, both the Democrats and the Republican claimed victory when both sides claimed to have won the Southern states of South Carolina, Louisiana, and Florida. This dispute was ultimately settled in early 1877 by what became known as the compromise of 1877. The Southern Democrats agreed that Republican Rutherford Hayes would become president and in return would remove all federal troops from the three Southern states. This agreement in essence ended the greater Reconstruction era and was the beginning of much harder times for blacks.

The Reconstruction started with so much promise for African Americans. All through the violence and intimidation by white terrorist groups, African Americans managed to vote and win political offices in many places in the South. Now this progress was about to be swept away. There was one area in which African Americans made significant and irreversible progress during this period: education. At the end of the American Civil War in 1865, only about 5 percent of blacks could read and write. By 1870 this literacy rate increased to about 20 percent. Many schools and colleges for blacks were established, and the quest for knowledge pointed to a much better future.

1877 TO 1914: BUILDING A FOUNDATION OF FREEDOM

When the last federal troops left the Southern states in 1877, the South began its consolidation of state's rights power. It was a plan to push African Americans back into everything that resembled slavery, a kind of de facto slavery.

Even during the active Reconstruction period, with the presence of federal troops in the Confederate states, there was a lot of violence, intimidation, and killing of blacks. Now, with no federal troops to offer any protection to blacks, white-supremacy terrorist and hate groups stepped up the attacks. With the blessing and even the participation of law enforcement, these groups had no restraint, and blacks, without protection from law enforcement, were on their own to protect themselves.

All the southern states passed what became known as the Jim Crow laws. These were segregation laws for all public places, including transportation, schools, libraries, universities, and parks. Private businesses and other white-owned groups and organizations also practiced the same segregation policies. The states made law that disenfranchised blacks at the voting polls with poll taxes, literacy tests, and other laws that kept blacks from voting. The US Supreme Court was very helpful to the southern states in their assault on blacks by issuing rulings that all but eliminated the Fourteenth Amendment for equal protection and the Fifteenth

Amendment for the right to vote. Most northern states were practicing the same discrimination as the southern states, but without explicitly stating so in their laws. It would take until the 1950s for blacks to only start to obtain their rights afforded by the Fourteenth and Fifteenth Amendments.

At the end of the American Civil War, newly freed blacks were without money, property, and jobs and had no way of making a living except by assistance from the federal government. The federal government urged black families to become sharecroppers and helped to negotiate contracts between landowners and sharecroppers. While the sharecropping idea provided jobs for blacks, it was not a good thing for them. The combination of illiterate tenants and dishonest landlords resulted in tenants becoming highly indebted to their landlords. With the tenants relying upon landlords for seeds to plant, equipment, and farm animals, as well as food and housing, it was very easy to manipulate the accounting. Most states' local governments had laws requiring blacks to have jobs or they could be arrested for vagrancy. Blacks could also be arrested for being in debt. This combination—reliance on landlords, plus the unfair laws—resulted in tenants being completely under the control of landlords. Very few blacks were able to prosper or to free themselves from the hold of their landlords.

The so-called justice system also played a role in this re-enslavement process. Black were arrested unfairly and sentenced to time in prisons and on chain gangs. Once in this system, blacks were forced to become free labor on both public and private projects and farms. It was very difficult for able-bodied inmates to be fairly released due to additional time sentencing and non-parole.

Despite all the difficulties and obstacles during this period, blacks were able to establish a foundation to build their lives upon as free people. Important areas were urbanization, education, business and professions, religion, music and dance, and life in general.

At the end of the American Civil War, most blacks lived in the South and most of them lived in rural areas. Almost immediately after the war, many blacks began to move to Kansas and other midwestern territories.

The trend continued during this foundation period. Many blacks moved to cities and towns as working opportunities became available, including into northern cities. Many all-black towns were established also. This urbanization movement would continue.

Significant educational progress was made during the period as more schools and colleges became available to blacks. The literacy rate increased to about 60 percent, and many more blacks attended and graduated from college. Many educational leaders emerged. Booker T. Washington and W. E. B. Du Bois were and are the most noted from the period.

Tremendous strides were made in business and professions. With the urbanization of blacks came markets for new products and services. Barber shops, beauty salons, banks, insurance companies, newspapers, retailers, and manufacturers are some of the new black businesses. Professional services, from black doctors and nurses to lawyers and other professionals, also became available.

Religion and the black church also changed. Many newer and better constructed churches were built. New religious denominations began. Newer forms of gospel music became famous.

Black music emerged from the shadows and moved into the larger America. Blues, gospel, and jazz, the foundations of American music, were black creations. Ragtime syncopation became the most popular dance music. Black dances also became mainstream. Classical music composition and performances were also done by blacks.

1914 TO 1918: WORLD WAR I

World War I gave many blacks the opportunity to move from the South to northern and midwestern cities. This period is often referred to as the Great Migration, when more than half a million blacks left the South for new jobs in the North. This increased urbanization by blacks was merely a continuation of the movement that started just after the end of the American Civil War.

In May 1916 the United States officially entered the war. More than 350,000 African Americans would join or be enlisted in the US Army. Segregation policies and southern officers made it hard for the black soldiers. However, the international exposure for the soldiers would pay dividends later.

1919 TO 1930: CONTINUING PROGRESS AND THE HARLEM RENAISSANCE

With the move of many more blacks to large cities, higher education, better jobs, World War I participation, and other intangibles, blacks, including southern blacks, were becoming more confident and proud as they felt that they were defining themselves as a people. Continuing migration and the prosperity of the roaring twenties aided this improvement.

The summer of 1919, however, was a very ugly time in African American and American history. Blacks were attacked by white mobs in more than thirty-six cities between April and October, and more than one hundred blacks were murdered. With little to no protection from local, state, and federal law enforcement, blacks fought back to protect themselves. Very few whites were arrested or charged, even though many blacks were, with some blacks even convicted and executed for protecting themselves. There were many reasons given for the riots, and newspapers and President Woodrow Wilson published many "reasons," all blaming this on black activity in Russian communism, or red-baiting. However, when all of the so-called reasons are peeled away, it was just racism, plain and simple.

The Harlem Renaissance of the 1920s and extending into the early 1930s was a very significant phenomenon for African Americans. It was a culture that showed the new Negro in full view, not just to Harlem and the United States but to the world. Great black musicians, writers, poets, scholars, actors and actresses, publishers, painters, and world-class businessmen were all part of this great renaissance. The history of the Harlem Renaissance is a must-read discovery for blacks interested in the details of African American history.

1930 TO 1939: THE GREAT DEPRESSION

In 1929 the roaring twenties came to a halt with the stock market crash that began on October 24, 1929. Panic, bank runs, bank failures, business failures, high unemployment, and many other negative events soon followed. This was the start of the Great Depression. Some scholars and economists believe that the stock market crash did not cause the depression, but most agree that the 1929 crash was the start of it.

Herbert Hoover, a Republican, was the US president in 1929. His tactics to deal with the depression were to raise interest rates and increase import tariffs. The overall unemployment rate increased from 3.2 percent in 1929 to 24 percent in 1932. Consequently, Hoover was defeated badly by Franklin D. Roosevelt, a Democrat, in the presidential election of 1932.

Blacks suffered greatly during the Great Depression, with unemployment rates twice that of the overall, around and greater than 50 percent in some cities. Historically black-held jobs were taken away and given to whites. Many black-owned businesses failed. The Agricultural Adjustment Administration (AAA) of the New Deal policies paid farmers not to grow crops so prices would increase. This resulted in an estimated two hundred thousand black sharecropper families losing employment.

In the midst of all the pain, two people brought great joy and pride to blacks and were seen as great gains for the race. Jessie Owens won four gold medals in the 1936 Olympics in Berlin, Germany. It was an embarrassment to Adolf Hitler and his Nazi white-supremacy propaganda. Joe Lewis won the World Heavyweight Boxing Championship in June 1937 and avenged a previous loss to German Max Schmeling in June 1938 by knocking him out in the first round.

1939 TO 1945: WORLD WAR II

In September 1939 Hitler and the Nazis invaded Poland and started World War II. This would also be the end of the Great Depression, as the United States and other nations prepared for war. Initially, the United States remained neutral and did not enter the war, although it was a major supplier to the Allied Forces of Britain, France, and other western European countries.

The defense industry created lots of jobs in the United States beginning in 1939. These jobs and other employment opportunities allowed blacks to migrate from the South to northern and western cities. Widespread racial discrimination in the defense industry resulted in very few blacks being employed. In 1940, blacks began widespread protest to the government for this employment discrimination, but with very little success. In 1940, A. Phillip Randolph, organizer and president of the Brotherhood of Sleeping Car Porters union, issued a threat for a march of one hundred thousand blacks on Washington, DC, in November 1941 if defense-industry employment discrimination and segregation in the armed forces were not ended. In mid-1941 President Roosevelt issued an executive order requiring fair employment practices in the defense industry. But segregation in the armed forces was not ended. That would not come until after the war.

On December 7, 1941, the Japanese attack on the Pearl Harbor naval shipyard resulted in the United States entering the war. Blacks were skeptical about serving in the war, as they remembered service in World War I and getting the same old treatment when they returned home. However, after several national black leaders came out in support of the war, black soldiers became more supportive.

At the start of World War II, all branches of the armed forces were segregated. Black servicemen were limited to menial roles, and few to no black officers existed. During the war blacks were able to get more officer commissions, including as pilots—especially the Tuskegee Airmen—as well as expanded roles for black soldiers. The war ended for the United States in September 1945, when the Japanese surrendered. Overall, World War II allowed blacks to increase their national and international status.

1946 TO 1955: MAKING PROGRESS DURING THE COLD WAR

In March 1946 Winston Churchill, the prime minister of Great Britain, gave a speech and referred to the separation in ideology between the communist countries of Russia and its allies versus that of the United States, Britain, and western European countries as the "iron curtain." This speech is often referred to as the start of the Cold War between communism and democracy, especially between the two most powerful countries, Russia and the United States. The Cold War became the most important agenda for the US government and the nation. Blacks were forced to make progress against this backdrop.

At the end of the war, black veterans were more confident than ever about themselves and their citizenship rights, but when they tried to exercise these rights, they met extreme opposition from white supremacists. Many black veterans were killed—with not a single person being charged.

In April 1945 Vice President Harry Truman became president when President Franklin D. Roosevelt died. In October 1947 President Truman's Committee on Civil Rights issued a report titled "To Secure These Rights." The report outlined four essential rights:

1. The right to safety and security of the person
2. The right to citizenship and its privileges
3. The right to freedom of conscience and expression
4. The right to equality of opportunity

The report also spelled out the government's role in ensuring that its citizens (especially blacks) obtain these rights. Truman passed the report to Congress and asked that it be implemented. Southern Congressmen objected, and nothing was done. In response to the inactivity, Truman issued Executive Order 9981 on July 26, 1948, to end segregation in the military. Although the report's recommendations were never enacted, it would become a very important reference document for black rights.

The presidential race of 1948 saw two factions split from the Democratic Party: the Progressive Party of liberals headed by Henry Wallace and the States Rights Democratic Party, or Dixiecrats, headed by Strom Thurmond. Wallace campaigned for civil rights for blacks. However, many of his supporters were communists, and thus his party was doomed in this Cold War, red-baiting time. The Democrats adopted a civil-rights plank during the convention. The southern wing of the party stormed out of the convention and formed the Dixiecratic party. President Truman won reelection, defeating Republican Thomas Dewey in an upset.

In 1951 William Patterson and Paul Roberson filed the civil rights petition, "We Charge Genocide to the United Nations (UN). This document charged that federal, state, and local governments were complicit in the murder, rape, and beatings of hundreds of blacks from 1946 to 1950. It documented the cases of many injustices with no one being charged and the federal government's refusal to pass a law against lynching. Although the US government was successful in its work behind the scenes to stop the petition from coming before the UN Council, it was an important and official document before the world that placed the United States on the defense regarding its claim as the leader of the "free" world.

In April 1947, Jackie Robinson became the first black player in Major League Baseball, playing for the Brooklyn Dodgers of the National League (NL). Robinson was a great player and a dignified and unquestionable gentleman. He went on to have an outstanding career. During his ten years in Major League Baseball (1947 to 1956), some of his accomplishments were NL Rookie of the Year in 1947; NL Player of the Year in 1949; six-time all-star; Six World Series, winning in 1955; two-time NL stolen-base title winner; one NL batting title; and a lifetime .311 batting average. All of this was accomplished while being subjected to the most intense pressure and scrutiny from the whole world. While Jackie Robinson achieved much personal success, he was many times more significant to the black race and its push for civil rights. Baseball was the American pastime, and to have a great black player in the world's spotlight was very important. The importance of Jackie Robinson to the struggles of blacks during the time cannot be overstated.

On May 17, 1954, the US Supreme Court issued its landmark decision in *Brown v. Board of Education*. The court's decision was unanimous (nine to zero) that segregated schools are unequal and thus a violation of the equal-protection clause of the Fourteenth Amendment to the US Constitution. This decision overturned the 1896 Supreme Court's decision in *Plessy v. Ferguson* that allowed separate but equal. The *Brown* decision was the crowning achievement of the NAACP's legal strategy to outlaw segregation in public schools. This strategy began in 1939 with Charles Hamilton Houston and ended with Thurgood Marshall as chief legal counsel in the *Brown* case. Marshall was a giant of a man in The Civil Rights Movement. His life history is a good study.

1955 TO 1965: CIVIL RIGHTS DECADE

White resistance to desegregation called for in the 1954 Supreme Court's decision in *Brown v. Board of Education* was swift and massive. There was much more "white flight" to suburbs to avoid integrated schools. Many local school boards gave public-education money to white private schools. Many states vowed to resist the law. These were just a few of many tactics used. In 1955 the Supreme Court issued a decision in the *Brown* case (often referred to as *Brown II*) that the states can proceed in integrating school with "all deliberate speed." This decision allowed states to really slow down if not stop the process altogether. It would take many years and many fights to achieve any substantial school desegregation.

In December 1955, on a crowded bus in Montgomery, Alabama, Rosa Parks refused to give up her seat in the black section to whites boarding the bus and was arrested for disobeying the bus driver's order. Rosa Parks was a model citizen, and the Women's Political Council (WPC) and the NAACP thought she was an excellent candidate to test the segregation practices of the Montgomery bus system. The WPC organized a boycott of the bus system by all blacks. After a very successful first-day boycott, a group met at the Dexter Avenue Baptist Church in Montgomery to discuss the boycott. They agreed to continue the boycott and created a new group, the Montgomery Improvement Association (MIA), to manage the boycott moving forward. Martin Luther King Jr., the new pastor of Dexter Avenue Baptist Church, was elected president of the MIA.

The boycott became a favorite nationally televised news story for all the national networks. Martin Luther King Jr. was a very articulate and charismatic spokesman, and he was often seen and quoted in televised coverage, all of which raised his national identity and profile. The boycott would last for 381 days and result in the Montgomery bus system's becoming integrated.

The 1957 Central High School integration case of Little Rock, Arkansas, was another highly visible civil rights case. On September 4, 1957, before a white mob of an estimated one thousand people, nine black children were denied entrance to Central High School by the Arkansas National Guard as ordered by Arkansas Governor Faubus. The federal government asked the governor to stop interference with the integration of the school. President Eisenhower ordered the US Army to escort the nine students into the school, and on September 25, 1957, the students entered the school. Again, all of this was covered on national television. The nine students would endure many insults and sometimes violence during school.

Martin Luther King Jr. may be the most important, most effective, and most influential person in the history of black Americans. After the successful nonviolent boycott of the Montgomery bus line, King came to believe that nonviolent resistance and protest could be the key to defeating segregation and obtaining black civil rights. In January 1957 King and some other ministers and activists created the Southern Christian Leadership Conference (SCLC) for the purpose of bringing the power of the black church to nonviolent civil disobedience and to assist blacks in their struggle for justice and civil rights. King became the first president of SCLC and held the presidency until his death in 1968.

The speeches, writings, and appearances of King are vast and legendary. During this civil rights era, the major civil rights engagement of King and SCLC are listed below in somewhat chronological order.

1. The Albany, Georgia, movement for desegregation in 1961 and 1962
2. The 1963 Birmingham, Alabama, movement against racial segregation and economic injustices. Television coverage showed demonstrators, including children, being attacked by police dogs and sprayed by water cannons

3. The September 15, 1963, bombing of the Sixteenth Street Baptist Church that resulted in killing four little girls during Sunday school was a major turning point for civil rights
4. The August 1963 march on Washington, DC, and King's "I Have a Dream" speech
5. The 1964 St. Augustine, Florida, movement
6. The 1964 and 1965 Selma, Alabama, movement for voter registration

In 1960 some students from North Carolina A&T University, a predominantly black college in Greensboro, North Carolina, began sit-ins at segregated lunch counters in Woolworth department stores. The sit-in tactics were extended to other stores, libraries, parks, and other public places. Sit-ins also started up in Nashville, Tennessee, and other black college cities. In April 1960 Ella Baker of SCLC headed a meeting at Shaw University in Raleigh, North Carolina, with black colleges' student leaders. The result of this meeting was the formation of the Student Nonviolent Coordinating Committee (SNCC) as a separate organization. SNCC continued to sponsor sit-ins and to give support to other civil rights agencies.

The Congress of Racial Equality (CORE) was formed in Chicago in 1942 by James L. Farmer Jr. and others. In 1961 CORE sponsored "freedom rides" to protest segregation in public interstate transportation, primarily on Greyhound and Trailways buses and in their bus terminals. These freedom rides resulted in many riders being beaten and jailed. However, it did draw attention to the problem. In 1964 CORE participated in Freedom Summer with SNCC and the NAACP to educate and register voters in the South. On June 21, 1964, CORE civil rights activists James Chaney, Andrew Goodman, and Michael Schwerner were murdered by Ku Klux Klan members in Philadelphia, Mississippi. Two of the civil rights workers killed were white, and this became an important point in the fight for civil rights, as now many more whites became supporters for civil rights for blacks.

Historically, the NAACP favored lawsuits and negotiation to achieve civil rights. Although the NAACP gave legal support to the other civil rights organizations, the organization itself was not highly active in the direct actions of The Civil Rights Movements.

Two *major* victories of The Civil Rights Movement for blacks were the Civil Rights Act of 1964 and the Voting Rights Act of 1965. The Civil Rights Act contained the following key items:

1. Banned unequal application of voter-registration requirements
2. Outlawed discrimination based on race, color, religion, sex, or national origin in employment and public accommodations
3. Eliminated state and local government laws that required such discrimination
4. Encouraged the desegregation of public schools and empowered the Attorney General of the United States to enforce integration
5. Expanded the role of the federal Civil Rights Commission
6. Prevented discrimination by race, color, religion, sex, or national origin by anyone who receives federal funds

The key provisions of the Voting Rights Act were:

1. Eliminated poll taxes, literacy tests, and other subjective voter tests or requirements
2. Allowed federal supervision of voter registration in districts where discrimination occurs
3. If discrimination happened the Attorney General of the United States could replace local registrars with federal examiners

These two laws and their subsequent enforcement were the culmination of many years of suffering by blacks that included the most vile and despicable acts that any human being could ever do to a fellow human being—all done with governments that initiated, legalized, committed, encouraged, allowed, and ignored such actions. All this took place in a country that considered itself to be God-fearing Christians and lovers of freedom, and that held itself out as the model of democracy for the world. *Shame! Shame! Shame!*

1966 TO 1980 BLACK POWER ERA

The Black Power era was a very important time for black Americans. There is no clear point at which The Civil Rights era ended and The Black Power era began. During the mid-1960s, many civil rights workers began to question nonviolent action. In June of 1966, Stokely Carmichael of SNCC used the term "Black Power" with a raised, clenched fist. The term and the raised fist resonated with blacks, and this was the unofficial start of the Black Power era. The assassination of Martin Luther King Jr. in April 1968 was the event that pushed the Black Power Movement into overdrive.

The term "Black Power" meant different things to different people, from political power, economic power, protect power, to creative power. The different views turned out to be positive because all became areas of actions for blacks. The term was also controversial to many blacks and outright despised by most whites.

New black identity was an important part of The Black Power Movement. Blacks no longer accepted being called "Negroes." The new accepted names were blacks, African Americans or Afro-Americans. Blacks began to identify more with their African heritage. African clothing, art, and languages became popular with many American blacks. The "black is beautiful" part of The Black Power Movement was one of the most important.

Historically, beauty for blacks in America had been defined by white values. The "fair skin, straight hair, and keen facial features" definition of beauty was accepted by most blacks. "Black is beautiful" included black skin, broad noses, thick lips, and nappy hair in its definition. The old black notions of "light skin, keen nose, thin lips, and good hair" were eliminated. The Afro hairstyle became very popular as a testament to the idea that black is beautiful. This new definition of beauty for blacks became a very valuable racial identity and a source of pride that still serves blacks today.

The Black Arts Movement was another important part of The Black Power Movement. Beginning in the late 1950s and early 1960s, many black artists began to challenge the conventional white concepts for writing, poetry, music, and dance. This was the beginning of the Black Arts Movement. The movement came together nationally in Harlem, New York, in mid-1965 when black poet and writer LeRoi Jones (who later changed his name to Amiri Baraka) started the Black Arts Repertory Theatre. Although the initial emphasis was on poetry, theatre groups, music, and dance, writers, novelists, painters, and sculptors also became a part of the artistic movement. Additionally, black magazines, journals, and publishers were created.

In 1964 the Lowndes Country Freedom Organization (LCFO) in Lowndes County, Alabama, was organized for voter registration and used a black panther as its symbol. By 1966 there were several Black Panther groups for voter registration in the United States that were inspired by the LCFO. Unrelated to the previous Black Panther groups, in 1966 in Oakland, California, Bobby Seale and Huey Newton founded the Black Panther Party for Self-Defense.

Initially, the Black Panther Party for Self-Defense was formed to address local community needs, especially police brutality. Party members began to carry guns openly and also began to have open confrontations with the police. The guns and self-protection aspects of the party resonated with many young blacks, and the party grew and became national, with chapters in many larger cities. The confrontations with the police, as well as the FBI's general fears and suspicions, resulted in the FBI targeting the party with the infamous COINTELPRO (counter intelligence program). The FBI and local police outright assassinated many party members and killed and imprisoned many others. By the early 1970s, from a high of several thousand in the late 1960s, the party was reduced to a few hundred members.

Politics was another key area of The Black Power Movement. In November 1966 Carl Stokes was elected mayor of the city of Cleveland, Ohio, the first black mayor of a large city. (Richard Hatcher had become mayor of Gary, Indiana, days earlier.) Political opportunities were created, with a combination of black voter registration, whites moving to the suburbs, and the emphasis placed on Black Power. Many blacks were elected as mayors, councilmen, state representatives, and other local officials.

Enforcement of the Equal Employment Opportunity Act by the federal government allowed blacks to obtain jobs that were not previously available to them. These new jobs allowed many blacks to begin to enter the middle class. This produced a counternarrative that blacks could also obtain power within the system. In an indirect way, this new wealth and opportunity contributed to the Black Power Movement.

With newfound pride, personal identity, and self-confidence created by and during The Black Power Movement, almost all aspects of black life were affected in mostly positive ways. In addition to the above-mentioned areas, religion, women's rights, the armed forces, black studies and education, and black business were also affected positively. Although The Black Power era had a rocky and controversial start, it now seems to have been the perfect way to transition from the civil rights and Jim Crow era to a more inclusive era.

1980 TO 2014: FROM HISTORY TO NEWS

Most significant events in history require the passage of time before they are fully understood and the impacts are fully accessed. In most cases this is at least fifty years. This time period is called "from history to news" for this reason.

Beginning in the 1970s, a noticeable black middle class started to appear. This was the result of more college-educated blacks, affirmative-action hiring and federal Great Society programs. We saw and continued to see many blacks doing well. More than a few blacks have done very well, and some are billionaires. While this is good advancement, there is much work left to do. The percentage of the black population in the middle class is much lower than the percentage of the white population in the middle class. Also, the income and wealth of the white middle class is much higher than that of the black middle class.

Hip-hop was and is an important black cultural idea and movement. It actually began in the mid-1970s in the Bronx, New York, when young blacks began break dancing, DJ'ing, and rapping for entertainment. Hip-hop music and clothing styles were added, and the entire product became the culture of hip-hop. Rap, hip-hop music, became a best-selling type of music. Young black teenagers and young adults of this era are often referred to as "the hip-hop generation." Hip-hop continues to be a big influence on black culture as well as other cultures throughout the world. For those interested, the details and history of hip-hop are a very worth-while subject of study.

Ronald Reagan became the Republican nominee for president in 1980. His first speech after receiving the nomination was a "states right speech" given on August 3, 1980, at the Neshoba County Fair in Mississippi, the same county where civil rights workers Chaney, Schwerner, and Goodman were brutally murdered in 1964. This was an indication of the type of president he became after winning the election.

Reagan was a staunch conservative with a long history of attacking all progressive and liberal policies and programs. He gave a large tax reduction to the rich that would lead to the current large income-and-wealth inequality that we see today. He cut welfare and social programs, all but eliminated Affirmative Action, set back unionization, ignored racial discrimination, and supported many other antiblack policies and programs—in many cases with the help of a few so-called black conservatives.

The federal war on drugs actually began in Washington, DC, in the mid-1950s when there was no "home rule" and the city was run by the federal government with policies and oversight by Congress. In 1971 President Nixon began the national war on drugs as a part of his "law and order" election promise. Although Nixon started this war on drugs, it did not spiral out of control until the 1980s and it is still out of control today. First Lady Nancy Reagan began her "just say no to drugs" campaign in 1981. Drug arrests, prosecutions, and incarcerations began to explode from then on. Blacks in the inner cities became targets of this drug policy. In 1986 the crack cocaine mandatory harsh-sentencing law was enacted. Also, many blacks were imprisoned for noncriminal simple possession of small amounts of marijuana. The war on drugs really was—and still is—a war on blacks, and there is lots of evidence to show that this was the plan all along.

At the 2004 Democratic Convention in Chicago, Illinois, a young black Illinois state senator named Barack Obama gave a keynote speech that was well received. This speech vaulted him onto the national stage as someone of high potential in the Democratic Party. He eventually went on to win the 2008 presidential election and become the first black president of the United States.

As soon as Obama was elected, and much more so after his inauguration, we saw many whites, including members of Congress, state elected officials, and especially Republicans, begin an all-out attack upon him personally and politically. Republicans did everything possible to oppose, obstruct, and ridicule anything Obama tried to accomplish. Many citizens showed no respect for Obama as the president of the United States. Almost all of this behavior was racially motivated.

Obama ran a great campaign that promised hope and change, and blacks were very excited about the possibilities. However, Obama was greeted with the worst recession since the Great Depression of 1930s, with much fear that we could be headed into another depression. He did a good job of avoiding economic collapse and guiding the country back to a solid economic foundation.

Obama was reelected for a second term in 2012. He continued to do good things. However, with no help, and in many cases sabotage from Republicans and many in the press, it has been a challenge for all of us. The impact of the Obama Presidency on the country and on blacks in particular will not be clear until it's viewed through the lens of history. One thing should be clear and learned: *No president or elected politician can solve our problems for us.*

The 2008–2009 Recession that began under President Bush was one of the deepest, longest, and most severe recessions in the nation's history. Black people always suffer disproportionately more in recessions, and this one may have been the worst aside from the Great Depression of the 1930s. Nationwide unemployment increased from about 5 percent to a high of more than 10 percent during the recession. At the same time, the black unemployment rate increased from about 7 percent to a high of more than 18 percent. As further evidence of this "last hired, first fired, last rehired" suffering by blacks, the August 2014 unemployment rate over-all was 6.1 percent, with a white unemployment rate of 5.3 percent and a black unemployment rate of 11.4 percent. Black poverty rate has also increased substantially, especially among children.

In the news of September 2014, we see current challenges in terms of low minimum wages, police killings of unarmed blacks, "stand your ground" laws, and voter-rights pullbacks that add to all our other troubles. On the bright side, we are doing very well in sports, music, entertainment, and educational attainment, and we must continue this good work.

BRIEF SUMMARY OF OUR HISTORY

A brief summary of our history shows three distinct eras.

1. For 246 years, from 1619 to 1865, we were slaves and suffered much pain, disappointment, and heartache. We created lots of wealth and happiness for whites but absolutely no significant victory or advancement for ourselves. All were stolen from us by a so-called "legal system."

2. Next, for approximately one hundred years from 1865 to 1965, we were purported to be free but were living under Jim Crow laws, staunch racial segregation, few to no civil rights, and little to no protection under the law. In 1865 four million freed former slaves began their alleged freedom without food, clothing, shelter, education, money, or occupation and had to learn how to survive.

3. For approximately fifty years, from about 1965 to today (2015), we are supposedly transitioning to full citizenship and equality in an American society that's (hopefully) substantially free of racism and racial discrimination. While some progress has been made, there is much, much, much more progress required to reach our goals.

Our history is a history of survival (both physical and mental), progress, and achievements of a people so mistreated and downcast that their mere survival is a miracle and a blessing from God. But not only have we survived, we have exceled. There is, however, much more to accomplish. And we will need to come together if we the people, and not just the lucky few, will achieve our just due.

4

Where Should We Go From Here

As we consider this important question, it is important to point out that what is offered here is not pontification from someone claiming to know "all things black." The interest, aims, and objectives of black people are many and very diverse. All actions presented herein support this freedom. What we are looking for is the key actions that will allow us to become the best people we can be, both individually and collectively.

Where should we as blacks go from here? There are many different answers. Some typical answers are:

- We need to get more blacks into business.
- We should keep young black men from drugs, gangs, and violence.
- We should strive to become equal to whites in terms of income.
- We need to eliminate teen pregnancy.
- We need to get government reparations for slavery.
- We need to improve graduation rates in high school and college.

The list could go on and on. The response of most people to these answers would be, "Yes, we need to do that." If one item is accomplished, then the next item will need to be accomplished, and so forth. Everyone will have their own personal priorities for the items. But let's look at the big picture.

What do we really want? As adults we all just want to live free, happy, joyful, and purposeful lives in pursuit of our goals, dreams, and ambitions. Children just want to live loving, secure, happy, and playful lives.

Here are five things that must be present just to have the chance to live this type of life.

1. We need to live in a safe, secure, and peaceful world, country, state, city, community, and household. Good economic, educational, and cultural opportunities must also be readily available. If there are problems in any of these, happiness is threatened. This is not something that an individual can give himself. We must get this from each other and society in general. Each of us must do our part to encourage, create, and maintain safe, secure, and peaceful living.
2. Man is a spiritual and soulful being. A man must have a good inner spirit and soul to live a happy life. Growing up in and living in a loving, joyful, and peaceful environment leads to a better spirit. Belief in God and a higher power, along with religious principles, can be a key.
3. Character is an acquired and ever developing and ever refining combination of many values, including intellect, emotions, morals, integrity, and ethics. Good character, like a good spirit, contributes greatly to living a happy life. Character is a very visible and perceived part of personality.
4. Good health is also needed to live happily. Even if you're rich and driving a new expensive sports car, life is not very good if you're in poor health.
5. In today's complex world, education and knowledge are a must. Learning and adapting to all the changes during one's life also requires continuous learning. Wisdom must also be acquired from living life.

Where Adults Should go to Now:
As we look out in 2015 and beyond, these are the basic things and places to go that we need moving forward to become the best people we can be.

1. **Good health.** It is often said that "good health is the best wealth." Good health includes body and mind—emotional, physical, and spiritual aspects. It is better, easier, and cheaper to maintain good health than to try to get it back through treatment. Eating properly prepared nutritious foods in the proper quantity, exercise, avoiding dangerous things and conditions, eliminating stress, and having frequent doctor visits and checkups are key factors.

2. **Good parenting.** Parenting is the most important factor in determining how well a child is raised and prepared to enter adult life. It is also the most important factor in determining the type of parent that the child will go on to become. Parenting should start at preconception and extend through to adulthood with both parents. Love, positive attention, and protection make a strong foundation to build all the many other things that the child needs to live a happy, successful childhood and adult life.

3. **High educational attainment.** All children must attend and graduate from high school with good grades and ready for further study. At least 60 to 80 percent should attend college or a trade specialty school right out of high school, with at least an 80 percent graduation rate. A good percentage of college graduates should go on to attend professional or graduate school. Children who don't start college or trade studies right out of high school should look to attending part-time or later. Education should continue on for everyone in some form for life.

4. **High employment with higher income.** With higher education comes lower unemployment and higher wages. A strong work ethic and high performance will keep you employed during

downturns and also lead to advancements. Business ownership can also lead to better employment and income.

5. **High voter registration and voter participation.** This is the best way to have some influence in the political process, especially in local and state government where educational and school-board decisions are made. It is important to vote in all elections—national and local, both primaries and general—and in both presidential and nonpresidential election years. Politicians will change their messages and actions when they know that black people vote in large numbers.

6. **All family households with children headed by married couples.** Far, far too many black family households today are headed by single females. Fathers must have a very high sense of love, responsibility, and presence to the family. Mothers should place very high value on keeping the family together. Very low divorce or separation rates, along with the elimination of childbirth out of wedlock, are critical to success for the children.

7. **Live a joyful and happy life.** Many times we become so focused or stressed out that we forget that life is meant to be enjoyed. Joy and happiness are the best place to be.

Children, with the help and guidance of their parents, must prepare for adult life with the following:

1. Live a happy, joyful, and loving childhood.
2. Maintain good health.
3. Build good character, high morals, and social skills.
4. Develop a good spirit.
5. Get a good education, both formal and informal.
6. Eliminate teen pregnancy—both male and female control is important.
7. Avoid drug use and drug gangs.
8. Avoid all other crimes and association with criminals or bad situations and influences.

The above are the fundamental items for success. An individual, family, or child may have additional things that are particular to their situation. Other organizations or individuals may do some things that may overlap or complement the above "places." All good things are welcome. It is not "this *or* that," but "this *and* that." People that are already living in "the places" can be inspirational and helpful to others.

In summary: *We want to be a free, happy, joyful, healthy, spirited, educated, smart, high-achieving, crime-free people of good character.*

This is the best that we can be. This is a happy place to be.

5

How To Get To Where We Want To Go

In today's complex and ever-changing America, black adults will be presented with many, many challenges and opportunities. How do we get to where we want to go? First, look at the two obvious approaches: (1) continue as we have been, or (2) lobby or protest federal, state, and local governments to enact programs that allow blacks more opportunities.

Obviously, we have made great progress since The Civil Rights Movement. There are many wealthy and famous blacks. A black man, Barrack Obama, was elected president of the country in 2008 and reelected in 2012. There are many middle-class blacks. However, when we look at the total picture, we see poverty, high unemployment, low-wage jobs, poor housing, poor educational attainment, health problems, high single-mother households, crime, high imprisonment, and even more factors that are not good at all. To continue on as we have been is not a good option.

It is true that certain governmental programs could help blacks substantially. Good-paying jobs and prekindergarten programs like Head Start are examples of such programs. There are several things about even good governmental programs that are *not* good. You don't know if or when they will be enacted, and as soon as they are enacted, an opposition party will try to substantially reduce or eliminate them. While it may be good to try to get such help (every little bit helps), it is not a good thing to depend upon or wait for.

This brings us right back to how to get to where we want to go. Imagine a young black adult with drug addiction, or uneducated, or with a criminal record. Obviously the chances of success are very, very small. Even if the shortcomings are overcome, success will come much later in life and may be substantially reduced. Now imagine a healthy, spirited, educated, and motivated black child with no negatives or bad habits entering adulthood. The child's chances of success are very, very good. Even facing discrimination, setbacks, and other obstructions the child will most likely find success. Our children must begin adulthood fully or very near fully prepared with little to no negatives or bad habits. This is how we can get to where we want to go!

> *Our children must begin adulthood fully or near fully prepared with little to no negatives or bad habits.*

We, as parents, guardians, and relatives, can raise a new generation in which every young black child will start adulthood healthy, spirited, educated, motivated, and without any major negatives or bad habits. Then they, as succeeding parents, can do the same for their children. And the process will continue.

This will give every child the very, very, very best chance for success in life, regardless of circumstances and personal dreams. In approximately one generation, all problems can be solved moving forward. These prepared young adults will spread out and achieve in all types of occupations, professions, businesses, and in their lives in general. All the problems facing blacks will be solved by using the best and most effective solution approach: *avoid the problems*. Even when new or unique problems appear, prepared adults can deal with them effectively. *This is the best, quickest, easiest, most efficient solution to all the problems facing black Americans*. Other suggested solutions only address very small parts of the problems and for a very small number of people.

WHY SHOULD WE DO THIS CHILD PREPARATION?

During the civil rights movements of the forties, fifties, and sixties, blacks were not living in a safe, secure and peaceful environment. There was open, so called legal, racism, open personal attacks, and discrimination, and we had little to no protection from law enforcement or the justice system. Also, economic, educational, and cultural opportunities were very, very limited and in most cases nonexistent. This peaceful living with opportunities that we did not have is one of the five things that must be present just to have the chance to be your best self. Therefore, it was necessary to protest and demonstrate to get these problems solved—as we did. This was something that had to come from the *outside*, not something that we could give ourselves. Since the mid-1960s, with the passing of the Civil Rights Act and the Voting Rights Act and the subsequent back-and-forth events of the seventies, eighties, and nineties, we have improved the peaceful living conditions to about as good as could be expected—although they are far from perfect. Although there are and will continue to be problems and events to address, now is the time to move on from this issue as a priority. Regarding economic, educational, and cultures opportunities, these items will always be competitive for the better or best opportunities. Good preparation and the ability to be both competitive as well as to create these opportunities are required.

The additional things needed to have a good chance to be your best are good spirit, good character, good health, and good education. And the seven places to go to become your best are: good health, good parenting, high educational attainment, low unemployment with higher income, high voter registration and voter participation, all family households with children headed by married couples, and live a joyful and happy life. Not any of these items can be granted or given from the outside. All of these are things we must do for ourselves. While there may be outside help, it is on us as parents to lead and "make it happen." Education is a good example. Although we think of education as an outside provision, if a parent doesn't take charge of the process of their child's learning, the educational attainment for the child will most likely be greatly reduced.

Another reason, and pardon me for not being brief, is the lack of, or very, very limited, seamless assimilation of blacks into American society.

All white groups such as German Americans or Irish Americans became white Americans or just "Americans," as they are called. We remain "black Americans." From a glance, all whites appear very similar regardless of ethnicity. Almost all blacks appear very different than whites. When you consider the natural fear and anxiety of people when they see difference, and the history of racial prejudice and discrimination in this country, this color-blind society that you hear or read about will not occur anytime soon for most blacks, if ever. Therefore, blacks, as a minority group, must come together to help and support each other to establish a position of strength and become a confident, prideful, and prominent minority group.

Let's look at some key aspects of this parenting base solution approach in a question and answer format.

1. **What is the cost of this approach?**
   Answer: There is no cost beyond the normal cost of raising children.

2. **Is there any government approval, action, or support required?**
   Answer: No governmental approval, action, or support is required. As mentioned earlier, there are some government programs that are very beneficial to parents and children, but none are required for the success of this approach.

3. **Are donations from corporations, private businesses, or individuals required?**
   Answer: No. Donations are not required. Donors tend to want to change the message, and money tends to cause corruption.

4. **Are there income, or education-level requirements for parents?**
   Answer: There are no income or education requirements. All income levels and educational levels are welcome and can become successful.

5. **Are there any religious requirements or preferences?**
   Answer: No. Although most blacks in the United States are Christians, all religions are welcome. Also, most religions help to build character and spirit and can thus be helpful.

6. **Are politics or any political ideology involved?**
   Answer: Although most blacks are Democrats, no politics are involved.
7. **Are there any equipment or "tech savvy" requirements?**
   Answer: While a smartphone, computer, or tablet with access to the Internet could be helpful, these are not required.
8. **What locations can participate?**
   Answer: There are no location restrictions.
9. **What amount of time is required from parents?**
   Answer: Parents will probably spend very little additional time above the normal time involved in raising a child.

The fact that this approach will get us where we want to go is indisputable. Everyone has seen that well-prepared children almost always succeed. This is true regardless of income, educational, or social status. The most common reason for this success is almost always good, committed, loving, and attentive parents. Contrarily, children of poor parenting have a difficult time finding success, without regard to income, educational, or social status.

Now here is the *most important and essential key* to making this solution approach successful.

The actions must be taken in a powerful, participatory movement in which we take actions together.

Large and systemic problems cannot be solved by individuals acting separately. We are not trying to solve individual problems (although they will break out this way). We are trying to solve problems for a large group of people at or near the same time. When you use individual actions alone, it will not work for most people. It will take a very long time just to get very, very, very limited success. It should be noted that separate, individual actions and the "try to fix broken men" approach is exactly what we are doing today—and the results are not good.

There is another big reason for a *powerful movement.* We need the strength, motivation, energy, and assurance that come from the movement. *It is difficult, or perhaps impossible, to motivate and energize a vast number of people and maintain actions with advice, talk shows, sermons, seminars, social media, and similar communications.* This movement can become so powerful that it can seem like a living and breathing thing.

A movement is the essential requirement to solve the problems.

This is:

A movement for the redemption of black America by a commitment of every parent of black children to raise their children to be the best that they can be and to actively participate in the movement to learn parenting necessities and to improve parenting skills and practices.

The name of the movement:

The Redemption Movement: Deliverance for Black America

Redemption is the act of being or having been redeemed. To be redeemed is to be removed or liberated from a compromised or undesirable place or position. A movement is the actions and activities of a specific group to accomplish a specific goal or objective. Deliverance is the act of being or having been delivered or liberated. In summary, we are using the movement activities of good parenting to raise our children to be the best they can be. This will redeem or deliver them from the undesirable circumstances that heretofore, or up to now, have awaited them.

All parents of young children, expecting parents, and soon to be parents should support and participate in this movement. Currently there are approximately six hundred thousand blacks entering adulthood every year. With the movement, we can send *six hundred thousand* young blacks per year into adulthood, fully or near fully prepared with little to no negatives or bad habits. In short, we can reach every black child—and yes, we want *every* child. No other program can even think of this type of number.

WHAT THE MOVEMENT CAN DO

How many times have you heard or even said yourself, "Why can't this man or woman straighten himself/herself out." What we know is that this person is most likely in a difficult position as a result of inadequate parenting, and it will be very difficult for him or her to escape, even with good help. How many times have you heard or even said yourself, "Why can't, or didn't, his or her parents do a better job of raising that child." What we know is that many parents don't have the skills, commitment, or stamina to raise their children well. With the movement we can come together, help each other, and solve most of the parenting problems.

The current time has given us this perfect opportunity, with several key things coming together. First, we have energetic, enthusiastic, and talented parents and youth who are disappointed with the plight of young blacks, and they are committed to make and *be* the changes that are required. Second, we have a strategy of parental activism in the movement that can solve the major problems. Third, scientific knowledge of what is required of parents and children at each stage of child development is readily available. Fourth, communication (with computers, tablets, smartphones, etc.) is easy and very inexpensive. And finally, we have the leaders and infrastructure that can bring it all together and make it work.

What we have in this movement is the opportunity to help each other be good, loving, and committed parents that raise our children to be the best that they can be. The parents can both teach and show their children how to become good, loving, and committed parents. (Remember that "more is caught than taught.") We can cover the entire country at the same time, and this will solve all major problems moving forward. Parents are not asked to do anything other than raise their children well.

WHAT THE MOVEMENT IS NOT

1. This movement is not about reparations or money from any government, organization, business, or individual.
2. This movement is not against any people, group, religion, race, business, or organization.

3. This movement is not about anybody's job, career, community, or other possessions.
4. This movement is not about any type of politics.
5. This movement is not about news and publicity.

WHAT THE MOVEMENT WILL BE UP AGAINST

You may think that any such movement that's all about good and is not against anyone or anything will have very little opposition or enemies. However we know that this will not be the case. We anticipate that the below groups will not like the movement.

1. **Haters.** It is believed that about 50 percent of white Americans hate blacks, or have strong white-supremacy beliefs or strong anti-black opinions. This hate shows itself in many aspects of society and in many different ways.
2. **Wage thieves.** Wage theft is perhaps the number-one way used to get rich. Slavery, low-wage undocumented immigrants, and low-minimum-wage laws have been or are still used for greed. Anything that makes workers' wages higher or reduces the supply of low-wage workers is seen as a threat.
3. **Fearmongers.** Fear is a tool that is often used to manipulate and keep people under control. People are easily scared, even by irrational talk.
4. **Status quo.** Many people just want things to remain as they are—good or bad.
5. **Police and law enforcement.** Currently, police think they need criminals and arrests to feel useful and for job security. Prosecutors, jailers, bondsmen, juvenile systems, and the prison system, especially for-profit prisons, all want and need victims.
6. **Politicians and governments.** Many politicians and some governments, especially local, feel more in control with a misinformed or easily manipulated electorate.

7. **News media.** News people want and need good stories. It is very easy to become news fodder—with all the so-called experts, "we heard," "he or she said," and so on—that distort the facts and confuse people.

In most cases all the things that people do and say against us can be easily defeated or neutralized by just *ignoring* it.

THE ENEMY WITHIN

Our most powerful enemy, and the one that defeats us more than all others combined, may be ourselves. It is only natural to be apprehensive and cautious when confronted with something new. However, to make progress we must move beyond this state of mind. Here are a few thoughts, with comments, that some prospective movement parents may have.

- **It's not anyone else's business how I raise my child.** While parents are given wide-ranging freedom, society has a vested interest in your child. Imagine that you raise a drug dealer or killer. Society will be very negatively impacted. If you raise a clergyman or doctor, society will be positively impacted. The Redemption Movement greatly respects your freedom to raise your child; it is only there to *help* you raise your child to become the best that he or she can be.
- **I already know how to raise my child to become the best that he or she can be.** This is a very good position to be in. Most often this is the result of having been raised by good parents yourself. However, Redemption Movement participation will help with motivation, determination, and endurance. You may also be a big help to other parents.
- **I'm concerned about what others will think or say about my participation.** Your main focus should be on what's best for yourself and your child. Some people will always be critics.

- **My work schedule or other commitments take up most of my time.** Sometimes it will be necessary to make some major adjustment or changes. Raising your child well should be a very high priority.
- **I don't have the money.** Fortunately, money is not the reason for success in parenting. People often believe that having money *guarantees* good parenting. This is not true. Love, positive attention, and protection are keys to good parenting—and they're free! Look around and you'll see many successful parents who were "dirt poor." You can also see many rich parents who failed miserably.

IN SUMMARY

What a wonderful opportunity we have in the Redemption Movement.

1. It can definitely solve all the major problems that our children will face moving forward. The movement addresses all the problems, not on a problem-by-problem basis, but in a systemic way that's all-inclusive.
2. It's so simple and doesn't cost anything. This may lead many people to think that it will not work or to ask why no one has thought of or proposed this before. The idea of good parenting as key is not new, and it has been discussed forever. The key, and the contribution of this book, is that we need a *powerful movement* to bring everything together. Just like we used the central idea of nonviolent protest during The Civil Rights Movement, we can use the central idea of good parenting in a national movement and solve almost all of the problems that black Americans face as a societal group moving forward.
3. There is no need for marches, demonstrations, and arrests. We can quietly and without fanfare get this done.
4. We don't need any outside approval, comments, or financial support.

5. All parents can participate equally, regardless of income, education, location, or religious belief.
6. All other actions that are currently in use, such as mentoring, marches, and demonstrations, can be continued outside the movement and will be complementary to the movement.

Unlike The Civil Rights Movement, in which we all benefited equally from the actions of others, parents must participate to get the desired results for their child. Parents should not assume that they can be successful on their own. Imagine a "civil rights movement" in which every individual demonstrated and protested on his or her own. No success there.

Again, this is the best, quickest, cheapest, easiest, and most reliable approach for our deliverance. There is no political or magic-wand solution. If we want it done, we must do it ourselves.

This is such a golden opportunity that we should not let anyone, especially ourselves, stop our success.

6

How To Start The Movement

While it is great to know that a strong movement can solve most of our major problems, suffice it to say that knowledge without focused, determined, and successful action is useless. In life, excepting such things as general education, written tests, quizzes, puzzles, and so on, to know may be only about 1 percent of the solution; *doing* is the other 99 percent of the process. The most important thing is: we must take it to heart and GET IT DONE, DO IT.

First, let's review what we're doing—and why we must do it.

We are a minority group in the United States. In 2014 there were approximately 42.5 million blacks—or about 13 percent of the total US population. As a distinct minority group, we are hated, blamed, discriminated against, profiled, denied our history, unfairly arrested and incarcerated, targeted politically, and murdered by police. In addition, our ideas and our wages are stolen from us, our image is tarnished, and little to no credit is given for our accomplishments. Need I go on? We can protest, demonstrate, or beg for things to stop or change. But as long as we're in a weak position, the larger society and the news media will simply turn away. Even if or when something is changed, after a short time it will be back to business as usual.

When we raise our children to be the best they can be, this creates strong adults who will avoid or neutralize all the bad things.

The child-development stages from prenatal to early young adult will typically be nineteen to twenty-three years of "active parenting." The table below shows the child-development stages for the active-parenting period. During this period, parents must ensure that the child gets the key learning and development that are normally required for each stage, as well as protecting the child from negatives and bad influences. The child should also live a happy, joyful, and loving life with the family during the active-parenting period.

Active-parenting Period

Developmental Stage	Age in Years
Prenatal	-
Infant	0–1
Toddler	1–3
Preschooler	3–5
School Age	6–11
Adolescent	10–18
Teenager	13–19
Early Young Adult	18–23

A child is typically born into the home of an immediate family of parents and siblings. The child will grow up in the local community that the parents live in. Both the parents and the child will live within and upon a society of foundation and support as listed below.

Foundation and Support

- Immediate home and family
- Extended family
- Community
- Government
- Country (United States)
- World

The interactions of the parents and the child with the foundation-and-support items are very important. The *immediate home and family* of the child is absolutely the most important for and to the child. When this is good, the child has the greatest chances for success. An *extended family* of grandparents, aunts, uncles, and cousins can also be very helpful. *Community* includes the people, businesses, services, and facilities that the child and the parent will come in contact with and deal with. It includes friends, neighbors, neighborhoods, day care centers, babysitters, schools, schoolteachers, schoolmates, churches, employers, and coworkers. *Government* is the federal, state, and local government agencies and personnel. *Country* is the United States, and it includes the people, businesses, facilities, and infrastructure of national interface. *World* is, of course, everyone and everything else that is not the United States. Family, extended family, and community are the three foundation-and-support items that will have the most impact on parents and children and will thus require the most attention. However, the actions and inactions, along with their influences, of all six foundation-and-support items will require attention and management for the child.

The details of parent information, practices, and procedures will be provided within the movement. However, let's look at a few basic things for interest.

- I have previously stated that *love, positive attention, and protection* make a good foundation for successful parenting.
- Love is the most important thing in a child's life—at all ages, including adult. Parents (and close caregivers) must love the child. This love must be manifested in words, actions, and feelings, and it must be unconditional and true. The child must feel this love from within on a heart-to-heart basis. As you love your child, your child also loves you. As your child is loved, he or she learns to love others without any instructions—the best (and maybe only) way to learn this. Love is what leads the parents to do all the other things needed for the child.

- Positive attention is the great companion of love. It is not just general attention or negative attention. It is the caring, loving friendship, complementary sharing, and being there that make the child feel good and confident, with a healthy self-image and so much more. It gives discipline, obedience, and so much more to the child.
- Protection means many things to and for the child. It starts with the protection of the fetus during pregnancy, then comes protection of the baby's health and safety, and continues in various ways to adulthood. It is the feeling of security for the child in that it is protected from fear and other undesirables up to the time that the child takes on the responsibility. It includes protection from hunger and malnutrition, and protection of health and well-being. The child must also be protected from drugs, drug gangs, other criminals, and many other undesirable people and situations.
- There are many other important things, such as talking to the baby from infancy on, reading to toddlers, teaching alphabets and numbers early, and many more, including many social items. It is very important to start this early because so much is formed within the child at this early age. And when it is not done at this early age, it becomes very difficult, and in many cases impossible, to bridge this gap later.

What does it mean to be "fully or near fully prepared with little to no negatives or bad habits"?

- **Fully prepared** means capable and ready to take on the responsibilities and duties of adulthood. Although there will be much learning, development, growth, and change ahead, the child is ready to start this process on his or her own. This preparation must include:
  1. Good health with good health habits
  2. At least a good, basic, high school education (and graduation), and in many cases, college or trade education

3. Good character with high morals, spiritual values, and social skills
4. Good knowledge and sense of the society and settings that he or she must live in, with the confidence to start and learn to navigate the system
5. Selecting a good path on which to start his or her adult life, with initial goals and ambitions, for example:
    a. Enlist in the armed services and perhaps make it a career, or get out after the initial service and pursue higher education or job opportunities.
    b. Begin working in the profession or trade that he or she was educated for.
    c. Continue his or her education in graduate or professional school.
    d. Work in a particular trade or type of business, or eventually start a business or become self-employed in this sector.
    e. Seek to get a job in this trade or type of business to develop the skills and learn the business.

- **Negatives** are self-inflicted things acquired during the raising of the child that will retard or put limits on the child's progress and accomplishments as an adult. Some examples are:
    1. Criminal record
    2. Teen pregnancy or young child out of wedlock
    3. Bad health problems
    4. Bad attitude or poor emotional control
    5. Gang membership—present and past—or association with other potentially dangerous influences and situations
    6. Addiction to drugs, alcohol, or other chemicals

- **Bad habits** are obsessive acts that if done continually will eventually undermine progress, happiness, joy, and personal well-being. They are very similar to negatives except that they are not yet "fully attached" and therefore may be controlled and in many cases eliminated. Some examples are:

1. Drug usage
2. Excessive alcohol usage
3. Smoking
4. Excessive eating, or eating bad foods
5. Poor personal grooming and dress
6. Bad driving habits, including texting while driving and excessive speeding

While the writings about raising a child can make the process look long and difficult, it is important to remember that, as parents, you will be with your child anyway for the nineteen to twenty-three years, while all the time raising your child—well or not so well. If you raise your child well, it will have a profound positive effect on the child, both as a child and an adult. If the child is not raised well, the result will not be good. But let's not focus on the negative. I am positive that every parent—*every parent*—wants to and will raise his or her child well to become the best that the child can be. Also, it is much, much, much more fun, rewarding, easy, and economical to raise your child well than to not raise your child well. The whole process should be looked upon as a labor of love, joy, and happiness.

Now, here is the beauty and effectiveness of The Redemption Movement:

- It focuses attention on parenting, and this will create the higher sense of importance that parenting deserves.
- It gives good and correct education and facts to everyone and thus avoids misinformation, deceit, and confusion.
- It provides motivation, determination, and endurance for the complete active-parenting period.
- It provides a social framework for parents to share ideas, encouraging them to give and receive help to and from other parents.

- It creates a national platform on which the whole country can come together and multiply the effort with incredible numbers of success. This is how we will ultimately redeem and deliver six hundred thousand young blacks into adulthood every year.

MY ROLE MOVING FORWARD

As the author of this book, I realized early on that this movement has the greatest of potential while at the same time being of no cost and with little to no outside hindrance or required approval. In a small passage of time, we can eliminate most of the problems black Americans face. I have looked, looked, and looked some more, and I did not see anything that comes close to being this effective for so many people and in such a short period of time.

Because this movement can have such a vast, positive impact, it needed to be presented on a large scale and with a national profile. This is the reason why I wrote and published this book. I will continue to promote this idea for the movement. This book is initially available at Amazon.com in paperback and Kindle e-book formats. Later, the distribution and e-book formats will be expanded. I will also promote the idea on Facebook, other social media, and on my author's website, WadeLJackson.com. I see my role moving forward as more of a support role. The movement can best be started and managed by smart, young, energetic, black leaders.

HOW TO START THE MOVEMENT

Here are some suggestions on how to start the movement. The items are listed somewhat sequentially but not necessarily so.

- Promote the idea of what you're doing in a clear and concise statement. "We're bringing parents of young children together in a movement to raise their children to be the best they can be by preparing the children to begin adulthood fully or near fully prepared with little to no negatives or bad habits." There can and will be additional discussion around this key objective. But the central idea is important.

- Generate interest and support among young parents, their family members and friends, organizations, and the community in general. Social media (Facebook, Twitter, YouTube, and so on) can be used to generate followers, including contact information (e-mail addresses, phone numbers) for future actions.

- Get the national, regional, and local support of the Black Church (all denominations). *The Black Church is key.* It is the greatest institution in our history as well as today. Children raised in the church get great Christian, spiritual, and moral values. The Black Church has established leaders and more facilities than any other black organization. This can get the movement started most quickly.

- Establish a leadership committee or group, and select or elect a national leader(s). The national leader(s) should be influential and charismatic, with an existing national profile or with the capacity to achieve this influential national profile. An influential and charismatic leader(s) is *the essential requirement* for getting the movement started successfully. (Michelle and, or Barack Obama would be dream leaders—after completing the presidency, of course.)

- Develop the process, procedures, and small organization necessary to start the movement on a small or limited basis.

- Start the movement on a small or limited basis and then make any changes, additions, and refinements required.

- Build a national organization and roll out the movement nationally.

It is important to keep money out of the movement. All workers, including the national leader, should be volunteers. As the movement expands, there may be needs for small funding; however, any funds raised should be minimized and specific.

LET'S DO THIS!

The Beginning—Not the End

Bibliography

Adams, Janus. *Glory Days: 365 Inspired Moments in African-American History.* New York: HarperCollins, 1995.

Asante, Molefi K. and Mark T. Mattson, *Historical and Cultural Atlas of African Americans.* New York: Simon & Schuster, 1992.

Clinton, Hillary Rodham. *It Takes a Village: And Other Lessons Children Teach Us.* New York: Simon & Schuster, 1996.

DuBois, W. E. B. *The Soul of Black Folk.* Chicago: A. C. McClurg, 1903.

David L. Lewis, Editor. *The Portable Harlem Renaissance Reader.* New York: Penguin Group, 1995.

Horton, James Oliver and Lois E. Horton. *Hard Road to Freedom: The History of African America.* Piscataway: Rutgers University Press, 2001.

Horton, James Oliver and Lois E. Horton. *Slavery and the Making of America.* New York: Oxford University Press, 2005.

Jackson, Kennell. *America Is Me: 170 Fresh Questions and Answers on Black American History.* New York: HarperCollins, 1996.

King, Martin Luther, Jr. *A Testament of Hope: The Essential Writings and Speeches of Martin Luther King, Jr.* New York: HarperCollins, 1986.

Loury, Glen C. *The Anatomy of Racial Inequity.* Cambridge: Harvard University Press, 2002.

Obama, Barack. *The Audacity of Hope: Thoughts on Reclaiming the American Dream.* New York: Crown Publishing, 2006.

Obama, Barack. *Dreams from My Father.* New York: Three Rivers Press, 2004.

Painter, Nell Irvin. *Creating Black Americans: African-American History and Its Meanings, 1619 to Present.* New York: Oxford University Press, 2006.

Robinson, Cedric J. *Black Movements in America.* New York: Routledge,1997.

Shillington, Kevin. *History of Africa.* New York: St Martin's Press, 1995.

Washington, Booker T. *Up from Slavery.* Garden City: Doubleday, 1901.

Woodson, Carter Godwin. *The Mis-Education of the Negro.* SoHoBooks, 1933.

West, Cornel. *The Cornel West Reader.* New York: Basic Civitas Books, 1999.

Zinn, Howard. *A People's History of the United States.* New York: HarperCollins, 2003.

Author Biography

Wade L Jackson is a retired engineer and problem solver from American industry. He is a mechanical engineering graduate of Tuskegee University, an MBA graduate of Xavier University, and a licensed professional engineer with thirty-eight years of experience in industry.

Having grown up during The Civil Rights Movement eras of the 1950s and 1960s, he was a keen observer of the movements and has continued to follow the progress of black America. As an analyst and problem solver, his specialty is to uncover the small, simple, often overlooked, yet essential things needed to solve problems while considering the tools as well as the restraints for the solution implementation. He maintains that solution implementation is the most important thing a book can offer. This book, *The Redemption Movement*, presents simple actions for a broad solution to most problems facing black America.

www.ingramcontent.com/pod-product-compliance
Lightning Source LLC
Chambersburg PA
CBHW050606280326
41933CB00011B/1999